W9-BMP-659

EARTH'S LAST FRONTIERS

DEEP OCEANS

Ellen Labrecque

Heinemann
LIBRARY
Chicago, Illinois

To contact Capstone Global Library please phone 800-747-4992, or
visit our website www.capstonepub.com

Edited by Rebecca Rissman, Dan Nunn, and Adrian Vigliano
Designed by Tim Bond
Picture research by Liz Alexander
Originated by Capstone Global Library Ltd
Printed in China by CTPS

17 16 15 14 13
10 9 8 7 6 5 4 3 2 1

Library of Congress Cataloging-in-Publication Data
Labrecque, Ellen.
  Deep oceans / Ellen Labrecque.
       pages cm.—(Earth's last frontiers)
  Includes bibliographical references and index.
  ISBN 978-1-4109-6178-5 (hb)—ISBN 978-1-4109-6183-9 (pb) 1.
Ocean—Juvenile literature. 2. Oceanography—Juvenile literature.
I. Title.

  GC21.5.L27 2014
  551.46—dc23   2013012938

Acknowledgments
The author and publisher are grateful to the following for permis-
sion to reproduce copyright material:
Corbis pp. 5 (© Ocean), 6 (© Tetra Images), 12 (© Ralph White), 26
(© Jeffrey Rotman), 29 (© Ocean); Getty Images pp. 13 (Kenneth
L. Smith, Jr. /Oxford Scientific), 16 (Julian Hibbard/Photonica), 21
(Kevin Schafer/The Image Bank), 14 (Dana Stephenson); NASA p.
4; Nature Picture Library pp. 8, 10, 24, 25 (© David Shale); Science
Photo Library pp. 9 (B. Murton/Southampton Oceanography Cen-
tre), 15 (Gary Hincks), 17 (Planetary Visions LTD), 19 (Nicolle Rager-
Fuller, National Science Foundation), 22 (Science Photo Library
NOAA), Shutterstock pp. 7 (© ktsdesign), 18 (© C.K.Ma), 23 (© Vadim
Petrakov), 11, 20 (© kokandr), SuperStock pp. 27 (© age footstock),
28 (© Reinhard Dirscherl/age footstock); Design features courtesy of
Shutterstock (© Ana Vasileva).

Cover photograph of a fish shelter in a cave reproduced with per-
mission of Getty Images (© JCP van Uffelen).

CONTENTS

A FINAL FRONTIER

Oceans cover 70 percent of the Earth's surface. Yet, only five percent of them are explored. We know more about the planet Mars than we do about our own oceans. Let's learn all about oceans!

WOW!

Did you know that 94 percent of life on Earth is aquatic, or lives in the water? That makes the plants and animals that live on land a pretty small group!

WHAT ARE THE OCEANS?

From space, planet Earth looks like it has one big ocean. In fact, there are five oceans on Earth: the Pacific, Atlantic, Indian, Arctic, and Southern Ocean. The Pacific Ocean is the biggest and the Arctic Ocean is the smallest.

WOW!

The Earth is the only planet in our solar system with liquid water on it. The Earth is called the water planet. The other planets are made up of rock and sometimes gas, but they don't have liquid water.

WHY ARE OCEANS UNEXPLORED?

It is very difficult to explore the ocean because, on average, it is 2.6 miles (4.3 kilometers) deep. This would be the same depth as 11 Empire State buildings stacked on top of each other. Most of the ocean is also pitch dark, making it very hard to see anything at all.

WOW!

The weight of the water in the ocean causes a lot of pressure down below. Some animals, like this rat-tail fish, have **adapted** to survive in the intense pressure.

OCEAN LAYERS

There are three main ocean layers: the Sunlight Zone, the Twilight Zone, and the Midnight Zone. The Midnight Zone is so deep that sunlight can't reach it. This makes it completely dark and close to freezing.

Sunlight Zone:
surface–660 feet

Twilight Zone:
660–3,300 feet

Midnight Zone:
3,300 feet–below

WOW!

The Midnight Zone makes up 90 percent of all the oceans. Yet, less than one millionth of this zone has been explored.

HOT SPRINGS

There are places on the ocean floor where boiling water from inside the Earth **erupts** from **vents**. So far, scientists have only discovered about 100 vent sites. But there could be thousands of them waiting to be found!

WOW!

Tubeworms live near vents. They have no eyes, mouth or stomach. **Bacteria** inside them convert chemicals from the vents into food. The worms grow up to eight feet (three meters) long.

VOLCANOES

Volcanoes at the bottom of the ocean erupt when Earth's **crust** splits or moves apart. **Lava** rises from erupting submarine volcanoes and creates new ocean floors.

WOW!

Scientists estimate that there are 5,000 active volcanoes under the sea! When lava rises high enough out of the ocean, it forms islands.

MOUNTAIN RANGE

The longest mountain range in the world is at the bottom of the ocean. The mid-ocean ridge is 40,389 miles (65,000 kilometers) long and runs through all the oceans on our planet. The longest range on land, the Andes in South America, is just 4,350 miles (7,000 kilometers).

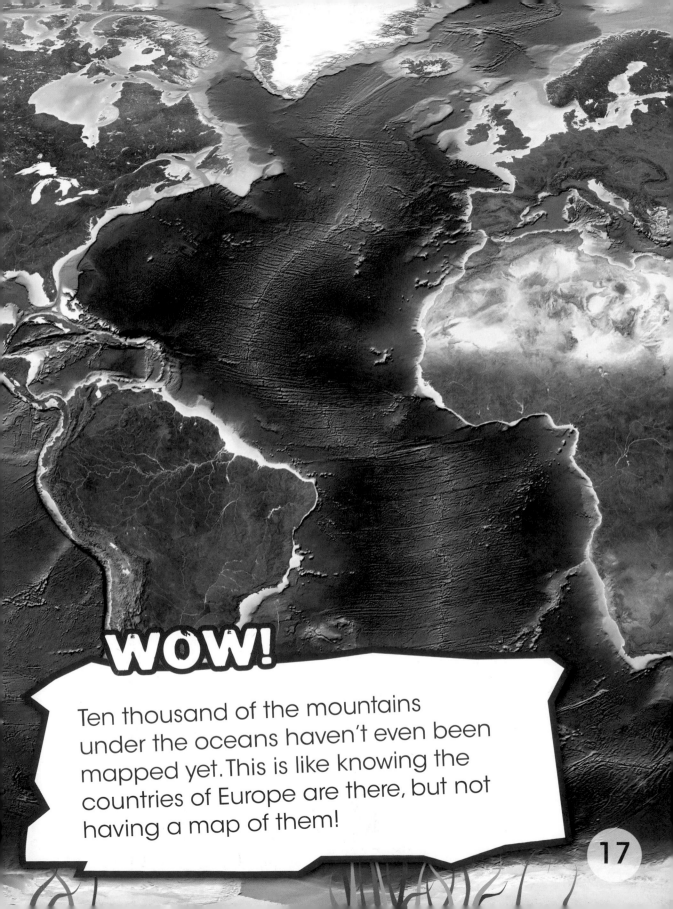

WOW!

Ten thousand of the mountains under the oceans haven't even been mapped yet. This is like knowing the countries of Europe are there, but not having a map of them!

LAKES AND POOLS

Scientists have discovered lakes and pools in an unusual place—on the ocean floor! These underwater lakes and pools are areas of very salty water. This means their water does not mix with the water from the surrounding ocean.

2.2 miles deep

WOW!

Lake Vostok is under more than two miles of ice in Antarctica. Scientists used a special drill to take samples of the lake water.

WATERFALLS

The largest waterfall on Earth is under the ocean. It was found under the Denmark Strait, a body of water that separates Iceland from the east coast of Greenland. This waterfall is about 2.2 miles (3.5 kilometers) tall.

waterfall

WOW!

The underwater waterfall is taller than Angel Falls, Earth's tallest land waterfall, by more than a mile and a half!

MARIANA TRENCH

The deepest place on the Earth is called the Mariana Trench. It is in the Pacific Ocean near the island of Guam. This part of the ocean has been visited and explored less than the moon's surface!

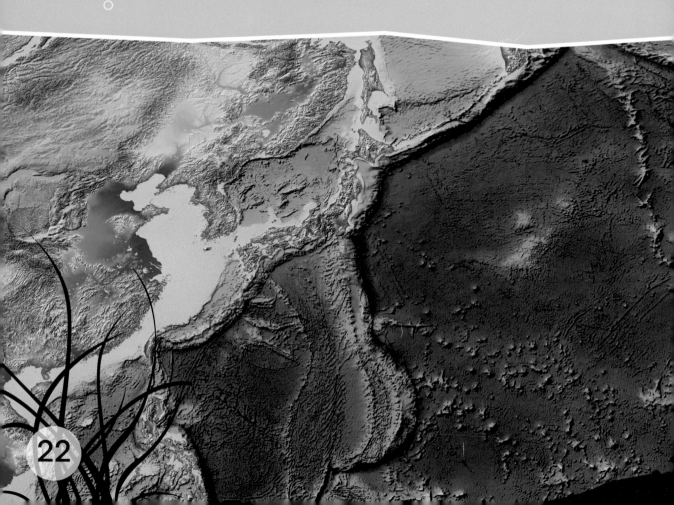

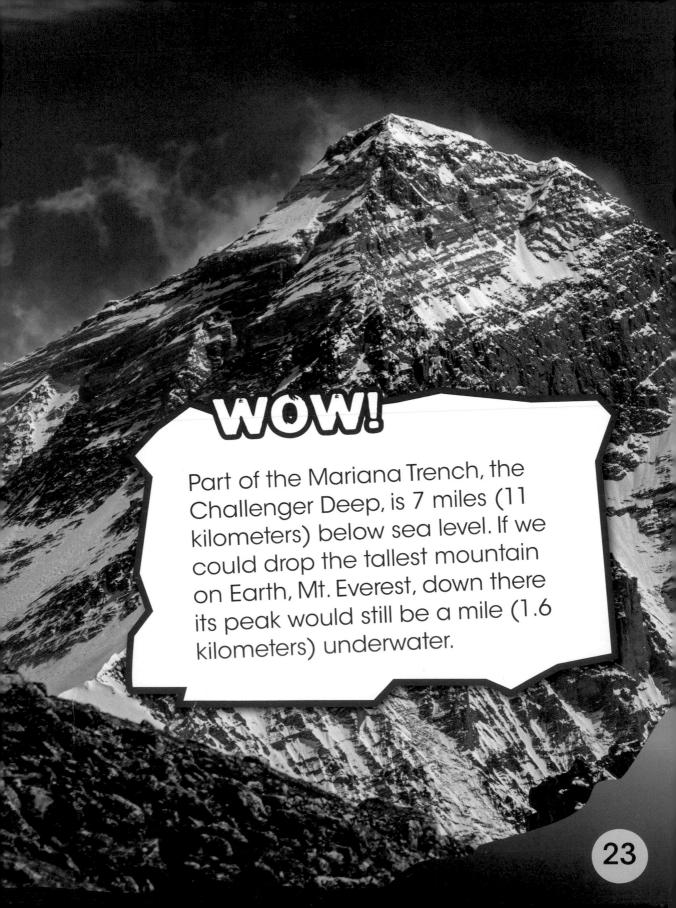

WOW!

Part of the Mariana Trench, the Challenger Deep, is 7 miles (11 kilometers) below sea level. If we could drop the tallest mountain on Earth, Mt. Everest, down there its peak would still be a mile (1.6 kilometers) underwater.

DEEP SEA CREATURES

Scientists think there are at least one million **species** in the ocean. But we have only discovered about 230,000 of them. Creatures at the bottom of the sea have soft, jellylike bodies. This helps them withstand the pressure of the water.

WOW!

Most of the creatures at the bottom of the sea have no eyes. Instead they use their other senses, such as touch, to find food in the darkness.

HOW WE EXPLORE

Scientists use submarines to explore the ocean. But the deep ocean is still too dangerous for people to visit often. Scientists often use robots and unmanned submersibles to study this cold and dark world.

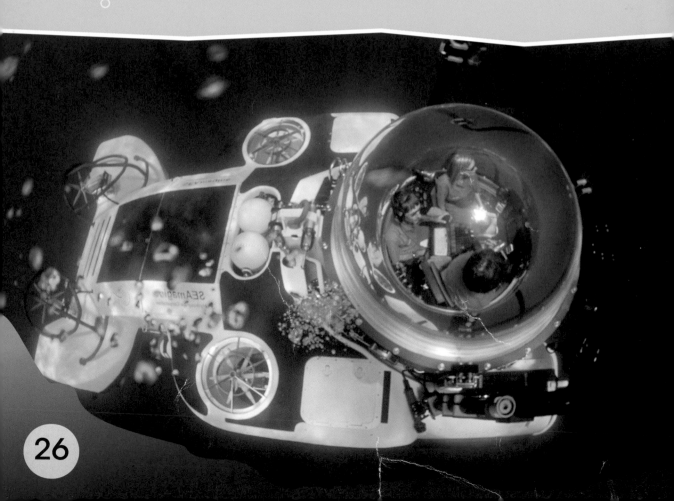

WOW!

Remotely Operated Vehicles (ROVs) explore the oceans by remote control. Using the remote controls, scientists can get the ROVs to collect plants and fish to study them.

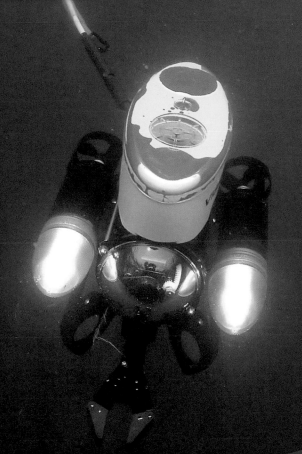

ONLY IN THE OCEAN

Oceans are mysterious and wonderful places. They are home to millions of plants and animals. The ocean can also be very dangerous.

It is our job to take care of the world's oceans by keeping them clean. Scientists continue to explore new places and discover more species than ever before.

GLOSSARY

adapted to adjust to new conditions

bacteria tiny single-celled organism. Millions of them could fit on the head of a pin.

crust Earth's outer layer

erupt explode or break open

lava hot, melted rock that comes out of a volcano

species living organisms that are very similar to each other and can reproduce

vents openings in the ocean floor where heated water shoots out

FIND OUT MORE

There are lots of sources with information about the deepest depths of the oceans! Start with these books and websites.

BOOKS

Hague, Bradley. *Alien Deep: Revealing the Mysterious Living World at the Bottom of the Ocean.* Washington, D.C.: National Geographic, 2012.

Llewellyn, Claire. *Oceans* (Habitat Survival). Chicago: Raintree, 2013.

INTERNET SITES

Facthound offers a safe, fun way to find Internet sites related to this book. All of the sites on Facthound have been researched by our staff.

Here's all you do:
Visit www.facthound.com
Type in this code: 9781410961785

INDEX